THE WAR OF POCKETS

The eternal battle between the "me of today" versus the "me of the future"

SUMMARY

ACKNOWLEDGEMENTS

Firstly, I would like to thank my wife for being my source of inspiration and constant support throughout the creation of this book. Your wise words and unconditional love brought these pages to life. This work is, in large part, an expression of our bond. Thank you for being by my side on this journey.

This book is a testament to the many inspiring conversations I have shared with dear friends, even as my name remains in the shadows. To the souls who accompanied me through the endless nights of reflections and ideas, your influence is immortalized in these pages.

Thank you to these incredible friends who have illuminated my path with deep insights and unique perspectives. Each dialogue was a gift, a source of inspiration that is reflected in the words that now unfold before you.

To those who, in some way, touched my life and provided me with the emotions and reflections that overflow in these pages, my eternal gratitude.

Every reader who chooses to explore this world I have created, you have made this journey meaningful.

May this book bring you joy, reflection and, above all, meaningful connections. Thank you for being part of this chapter of my literary journey.

With gratitude,

[A lover of finances and life lessons]

INTRODUCTION

Why waste your precious time on yet another personal finance book? I know, the last thing you need is another boring expert telling you how to spend your money. But before you close this book, give me a chance to convince you that the "War of the Pockets" is different. I don't promise magic formulas to get rich overnight, but I offer something just as valuable, a relaxed journey, full of practical insights.

You are browsing these pages not with the intention of delving into the intricacies of financial charts or deciphering the secrets of famous investors. After all, if that were your desire, you would be tuning into economic programs, starting college, taking a course or watching content from renowned gurus. Here, in the "War of the Pockets", our objective is completely different.

This is not another manual on budgeting and investing. Here, you won't find financial jargon that makes your eyes glaze over, but rather an accessible and engaging approach. I believe that learning about decisions and money doesn't have to be a chore. Let's uncomplicate financial complexities and discover, together, valuable perspectives that can emerge along the way, providing useful insights into our decisions.

The title of the book alone reveals the central theme: 'The Eternal Battle between the Present Self and the Future Self'. In this work, we will explore the decisions we make throughout our lives and their impacts on the future. We will look at the choices and options available in various situations, examining them thoroughly to understand the implications for both "current me" and in the "me that is to come". In other words, we will investigate the consequences of each decision, addressing both sides of the coin.

Plus, we'll delve deeper into the crucial differences between the external influences that shape our lives and the choices we consciously make. How can we discern between external pressure and the internal voice that guides our decisions? How does each of these forces play a role in the eternal battle between the present and the future? By understanding these distinctions, we will be better prepared to chart our path with discernment and wisdom.

We're also not here to judge your spending or dictate an austere lifestyle. Instead, I'm here to guide you on a journey of financial self-discovery, where we understand the reasons behind our spending habits and learn to balance the present with the future.

Here is an invitation to a relaxed journey, where wisdom does not come from graphs and technical analyses, but from laughter when faced with common decisions. The "War of the Pockets" is about learning to appreciate each daily choice, understanding that financial life can be as colorful as a palette of options on a restaurant menu.

Take a moment to relax and delve into the pages of "War of the Pockets". Here, we're not just aiming for a robust bank balance, we're discovering the value of every everyday choice and how it contributes to the unique narrative of your life. Get ready for an adventure where learning is easy, and choices, no matter how simple they seem, are real battlefields in the great War of Pockets.

The Call to Battle

You've probably heard a lot of this, but imagine yourself faced with daily choices: spend money on a coffee today or save for a trip next year. Choose to buy something impulsive or invest in something that benefits your tomorrow self. Ah, the eternal dilemma of coffee versus the next big adventure! It sounds cliché, doesn't it? But let's be honest, clichés exist for a reason. After all, who hasn't found themselves staring at the menu?cafeteria and thinking, "Hmm, if I cut out that cappuccino now, I could be enjoying a drink on the beach in a few months"?

This is the constant battle between Today's Self and Future Self, a struggle we all face on our financial journey, whether we want to or not. But don't worry, remember that we're not here to tell you to cut out your daily coffee.

The battle between the "Today Me" and the "Future Me" may sound like an exaggerated drama, but believe me, it is a spectacle that unfolds daily in our financial lives. Because, let's face it, we are all reluctant protagonists in this epic plot, where coffee and travel are the supporting characters in a story that we are constantly writing, whether we are aware of it or not.

As we face the crossroads of consumption, we are all like inexperienced generals on a financial battlefield, trying to decide whether to send our troops into the familiar terrain of today or invest in an unknown expedition into the territory of tomorrow. While some prefer to flip the coin to decide, the "War of the Pockets" invites us to be more astute strategists.

The truth is, when we face these internal conflicts, we are shaping the plot of our financial lives. Each choice, each renunciation, is a line in the script we are writing. And let's be honest, who needs a screenwriter when we're the improvised protagonists of this financial comedy? After all, we don't need someone telling us that changing our car for the latest model year or purchasing the latest cell phone is as rewarding as having a constant flow of money flowing into our account every month without us having to lift a finger, do we?

That's why I believe that the battle between the "Me of Today" and the "Me of the Future" is not about cappuccinos or travel, cell phones or investments, it is about self-awareness and the search for a balance that allows us to enjoy the present without irreparably harming the future. We may not have a treasure map or infinite money, but we can learn to navigate the uncharted seas of financial responsibility with a strong sense of strength.mental bulletproof.

So, dear reader, prepare yourself for the battles to come. As we dive into the next few pages, we'll explore smart strategies, laugh at financial pitfalls, and most of all, celebrate the small victories that bring us closer to the happy ending of a life well lived. Because, after all, in this "War of the Pockets", the true achievement is in the journey, not the final destination. Are you ready to move forward? The challenge is set, and the next page of this financial epic waits to be written. Let's fight!

Part I: Financial Roots in Childhood

In the vast landscape of our lives (and in the wake of the book), it is essential to understand the distinction between expectation and perspective, two concepts that shape different approaches toward goals. While expectations often lead us down paths shrouded in idealization and anxiety, perspective emerges as a beacon of clarity, guiding us through a terrain of objectivity and growth. This contrast between what is expected and what is possible forms the core of our personal and professional journey. When we better compare these two perspectives, we notice the change from a mentality focused on fleeting dreams to a more practical approach, based on the ability to adapt and internal control of situations.

EXPECTATION	PERSPECTIVE
The anticipation of the unknown	Clarity of the path to be followed
Uncertainty and emotion	Focus and objectivity
dreams and imagination	Realistic and concrete goals
Potential for disappointment	Growth opportunity
Idealizations and fantasy	Pragmatic analysis of reality
Anxiety in front of unknown	Confidence in adaptability
High personal expectations	Acceptance of limitations
Search for immediate gratification	Investment in the process
Positive or negative surprises	Strategic planning
Influenced by external factors	Focus on internal control

By analyzing the comparison table between expectation and perspective, we can draw some valuable conclusions about changing mindset and approach when facing unknown challenges and situations. Here are some conclusions that can be derived from the comparison:

Change of Focus

Expectation: Focus on the unknown and emotion.

Perspective: Focus on realistic goals and objectivity.

Perspective promotes a shift in focus from the unknown and emotional to tangible goals and a clearer vision of the path to be taken.

Adaptation and Growth

Expectation: Potential for disappointment in the face of surprises.

Perspective: Opportunity for growth through adaptation.

The perspective highlights the ability to grow and develop through adaptation to circumstances, transforming challenges into opportunities.

Realism vs. Idealization

Expectation: Idealizations and fantasies.

Perspective: Pragmatic analysis of reality.

The perspective encourages a more realistic approach, replacing idealizations with a pragmatic analysis of the situation, contributing to a more grounded understanding.

Internal control

Expectation: Anxiety in the face of the unknown and external influence.

Perspective: Confidence in adaptability and focus on internal control.

The perspective emphasizes confidence in personal adaptability and the importance of focusing on what can be controlled internally, reducing anxiety caused by external factors.

Process vs. Immediate Result

Expectation: Search for immediate gratification.

Perspective: Investment in the process.

The perspective highlights the importance of investing in the process, recognizing that lasting results often require time and ongoing effort.

These conclusions reflect the evolution from an initial expectation-based mindset to a more mature and balanced perspective. By taking a more perspective-driven approach, individuals can find greater resilience, adaptability, and satisfaction in their journeys.

Financial expectations often make us focus on quick results, seeking immediate gains. This short-term view can lead us to impulsive decisions, prioritizing accumulating wealth quickly, without considering the risks and long-term consequences. In this mindset, we are guided by immediate desires and seek quick results, without thinking about future implications.

In contrast to this approach, the financial perspective is like looking at the long-term horizon. Here, the focus is on building a solid foundation with solid investments and strategic planning. This vision values not only continued financial stability, but also encourages learning about finances, promoting informed and conscious decisions. By adopting this perspective, we understand the importance of adapting to financial changes, adjusting strategies to reduce risks and ensure stability over time.

Expectation is more linked to the search for immediate results and quick gains, while perspective adopts a broader view, valuing long-term stability.

Start of the Journey

Now, we enter the intriguing terrain of the "Me of Today", a set of impulses more immediate than a purchase made in the heat of the moment. These unruly impulses are like kids in a candy store, eager for attention and instant gratification. Even without fully understanding what they're doing, they're ready to shine, even if it's just for a few minutes in the checkout line.

Our mission here is as challenging as saying which came first, the chicken or the egg, or explaining the difference between simple and compound interest. We are dealing with a group that often acts first and asks questions about the results later. They are like impulsive little strategists, always ready to attack the wallet without considering the financial consequences, as if a battle plan were a relic of the past.

This behavior is not just a modern peculiarity, its roots can be traced back to the dawn of humanity. From the days when our ancestors traded resources to meet immediate needs to the present, where a quick click can satisfy our momentary desires. The story of "Today's Me" is, in fact, a journey that spans the centuries, with hints of impulsiveness that stand the test of time.

At school

The formation of this behavior was not an example of military strategy, but a natural response to a world that insists on telling us, "Buy now, think later." Every part of your "today self" has been shaped by the influences of modern consumerism, as if you have undergone intensive training in shopping temptations. Ever since we were at school, there was always that little friend with the trendy sneakers, the incredibly expensive backpack or the pencil case with the latest trend emblem. Who didn't want to be the highlight of the playground, showing off the shiny accessory that did everyone sigh? Or those sneakers that flashed and/or had wheels? Of course, even if, at the time, we didn't even know how to tie our own shoelaces.

Recess was like a silent war, where social acceptance was measured not by well-done homework or good grades on exams, but by the shiny items on display.we exhibited. After all, who needs good grades when you can have a pencil case so shiny that even teachers look away? And so, that desire to be the friend with the cool sneakers has stayed with us, growing and turning into shopping impulses that defy not only logic, but also your bank balance.

The formation of our expectations regarding consumption is deeply influenced by childhood, connecting popularity and social acceptance to material goods. Exploring influences from the first years of life is essential for a deeper reflection on the motivations that drive our consumption choices. Confronting this childhood legacy invites us to critical analysis, allowing us to more fully understand the factors that shape our consumption patterns throughout life.

In summary, the reflections in this report highlight the lasting influence of childhood on our consumption choices, highlighting the importance of self-awareness in the face of social expectations. A mature perspective involves transcending superficial materialism, prioritizing genuine achievements and authentic relationships. Balancing emotional impulses and financial logic is crucial in the adult journey, while reflecting on deep-rooted patterns allows for positive transformation. Thus, by adopting a conscious and reflective perspective, we can follow more meaningful paths in the context explored by the book.

First allowance(s)

The glorious moment when we hold our first bit of money, as if it were a newly discovered treasure! At that moment, we are faced with the first great philosophical question of childhood:

how on earth are we going to spend this fortune? The option to "save for more later" doesn't even reach children's minds. Kids are more like "buy candy now" or "invest the entire budget in shiny stickers", financial strategies that Warren Buffett might not approve of. And who can blame them? After all, saving for the future is no match for the instant satisfaction of a bag full of goodies. Because, let's face it, stocks and treasury bonds don't have the same excitement as a kinder egg with a surprise toy. And when adults say "think about the future", the child's mind responds with a resolute "but what if I never get there?" The first encounter with money is like a theme park of crazy choices, and children are the most fearless adventurers in this playful financial world.

In short, early experiences with money reveal a tendency for immediate gratification in children, while the idea of saving for the future is often neglected. This scenario highlights the need for an educational approach that balances the excitement of the present with the importance of conscious financial choices. The difficulty in making financial concepts attractive to younger people highlights the importance of engaging and clear educational strategies. By recognizing these dynamics, we can develop a more balanced financial perspective from childhood, preparing future generations for more conscious financial management.

The first transaction and initial choices

In this peculiar scenario, the laws of supply and demand are outlined in the exchange of playground cards, where the most desired chrome can be exchanged for an astronomical quantity of marbles. Children's entrepreneurial spirit also shines through, with small business owners establishing their lemonade "companies" or selling drawings, while competition for the title of "CEO of the Patio" reaches intense levels. Inflation, in turn, is revealed in the exorbitant prices of snacks in the school canteen, leading some to reconsider whether it is worth investing their entire allowance in a single chocolate bar.

Within this fascinating economic microcosm, a sincere question arises from children: "Why do I need to choose between the chocolate bar and the snack? I just wish I could buy both." This innocent yet simple reflection sheds light on the inevitable nature of choices and scarcity, even in the playful world of children's finances.

In short, childhood economic experiences, such as trading cards and small businesses, offer valuable insights. They demonstrate a natural understanding of basic economic laws, forming the basis for financial learning from an early age. Lessons about inflation, entrepreneurial competition, and the need to make informed choices contribute to the early development of essential financial skills. This context illustrates how childhood experiences influence the economic perspective, preparing children for a more conscious and insightful approach to finance throughout their lives.

Lessons that resonate in Adult Life

Consumer society

During the 20th century, societies underwent significant change, leaving behind old production economies and embracing modern consumer economies. This transition was driven by economic development, technological advances and marketing strategies that transformed the act of consumption into a desirable lifestyle. In short, buying things has become the biggest trend of the century, thanks to a mix of money, technology and advertising.

Impacts on the formation of "Today's Me"

We realize that the exchange of marbles, the lemonade deals and the decisions between chocolate bars and snacks are not mere passing episodes in childhood. They are seeds planted in a fertile soil of learning, destined to germinate throughout adult life. Lessons about the value of money, the art of negotiation, and the inevitability of choices shape not only playground play, but also the way we face real-world economic challenges.

In this childish scenario, where each candy exchanged is an economic transaction on a reduced scale, children not only explore the fundamentals of the economy, but also develop essential skills for adult life. Little Yard CEOs are unknowingly preparing for the corporate corridors and more complex financial decisions they will encounter on life's journey.

Part II: Following in the footsteps of youth

Television and brainwashing

Now, going a little further, as we enter the world of television, we realize that the war against impulse purchases has a new episode. We cannot deny that, since childhood, television commercials have been the master generals of this battle. They have invaded our living rooms, manipulating our desires and transforming ordinary products into priceless treasures. Who doesn't remember that toy commercial that, with a little song that lump in our heads, suddenly became essential to a child's happiness? Or that cereal advertisement that promised radiant mornings and epic adventures?

These advertising strategies were like intensive training for the formation of the "Me of Today", teaching us to desire things we didn't even know we wanted. And, of course, as adults, we still face the aftereffects of this television training. How many times have we caught ourselves thinking that the new version of the vacuum cleaner could actually bring genuine happiness to our lives? Or that the latest innovation in cookware could transform our kitchen into a gastronomic sanctuary?

Television is often the training ground where the soldiers of "Today's Me" are transformed into voracious consumers. They're not just products, they're dreams packed in shiny boxes, ready to be unwrapped with the promise of an easier, happier life.

The lessons learned from the impact of television commercials point to the need for a conscious perspective on consumption. Recognizing the manipulation of desires from childhood allows you to evaluate true needs, while understanding the lasting effect of television training empowers more critical decisions. Separating the emotional promise of products from their actual utility is crucial to a more pragmatic approach. In the face of ongoing challenges in adult life, maturity involves constant awareness, guiding purchasing choices aligned with personal values and a search for meaning beyond the material. Thus, the conscious perspective becomes a valuable compass on the journey outlined by the book.

Social media models

As we move forward on the topic of television influence, we cannot ignore the evolution of technology, which increasingly seems to play against it, now extends to social media. If television was the primary training school for the soldiers of "Today's Me", social networks have become the advanced academy, taking the war against shopping impulses to a new level.

Remember those commercials that convinced us to want products we didn't even know existed? Well, social media does this on an even more personalized scale. They study our habits, monitor our clicks, and suddenly our feeds are flooded with ads meticulously tailored to our most intimate desires. That jacket you didn't even know you wanted? Now it is essential to your existence, at least according to the algorithms. Have you ever stopped to think about that strange feeling of mentioning a topic, like marriage, in an informal conversation and then noticing related suggestions on your cell phone? Or when you excitedly share vacation plans with friends, only to receive suggestions for exotic destinations, often accompanied by tempting proposals from travel agencies that swear they will go out of their way to allow installments to be paid in 50 installments, making the getaway a reality, no matter what.

Just like television, social networks have transformed products into true icons of desire, packaged in narratives of happiness and success. Colleagues parade their latest achievements, and, without meaning to, we end up entering the frenetic rhythm of shopping, where social validation seems to be discounted, but still on sale. It's as if social media were the magical ticket to a dream trip to places we didn't even know existed. Suddenly, we're all exploring exotic destinations that seem straight off an imaginary map, where the only luggage needed is our imagination (and maybe a decent photo filter).

In summary, the lessons learned from the influence of social networks on consumption point to the need for a conscious perspective in a digital scenario. Understanding the personalization of influence, algorithmic manipulation, and the illusion of necessity empowers more thoughtful choices. Decoupling social validation from impulsive consumerism stands out as a priority, as does discerning between virtual exploration and material reality. By adopting a perspective that is resistant to the pressures of social media, readers are guided in the search for a balance between digital life and consumer choices aligned with their own narratives of happiness and success.

18 years old: "Adultization" - Hormones, driver's license (of freedom) and responsibilities

When we reach adulthood, we are thrown into a whirlwind of changes, a peculiar phase that I affectionately nicknamed "Adultization". This stage turns everyday life into a comedy, where youthful impulses dance along with newfound responsibility.

In "Adultization", we face the delicate balance between the search for the long-awaited financial independence and the temptation/need to continue counting on the support of our parents. This phase, full of experiences, propels us into the territory of adulthood, where the comedy of life unfolds between unexpected turns and humorous dilemmas in the search for financial autonomy, contrasting with the security offered by parents.

Responsibility - A Comic Plot of Becoming "Responsible"

The word "responsibility" in this chapter is like a stubborn character in a comedy. We are old enough to vote, but we still depend on our parents for financial loans. The fine line between youth and adulthood often feels like a tug of war, with responsibility pulling us to the side of commitment and hormones trying to drag us back to adolescence.

At the age of 18, we are faced with the challenge of balancing the desire for independence with the often limited financial reality. Although theoretically considered adults, we realize that life does not come with a financial instruction manual. At this crossroads, we deal with the task of managing money, paying bills and, at the same time, satisfying the youthful impulses that persist in accompanying us. The autonomy provided by adulthood becomes, in a way, a comedy scenario. We try to balance financial responsibilities with irresistible day-to-day temptations, such as deciding between an impulsive purchase or saving for future projects. At this stage, we learn to approach daily choices more consciously, recognizing that each decision not only shapes our present, but also sows seeds for our future.

Driver's License - The Key to Freedom

The search for a driver's license, a journey that often resembles trying to start a vehicle while comfortably in the back seat. Firstly, let's face reality: if your parents don't pay for driving school, the conversation about your driver's license won't even happen.start. But for educational purposes (and the content of this book, of course), let's pretend we all have amazing parents who shell out the cash to make our driving dreams come true.

Now, imagine the curious scene of you walking half an hour from your house to the bus stop, taking the overcrowded bus and subway, just to go to driving school. You invest precious hours of your life in intensive training, juggling learning the goal and controlling your nerves in practical classes, all in search of the much-desired driver's license.

After countless trips on crowded buses towards the driving school, added to the hours invested in intensive training to earn the dream driver's license, the final revelation is like discovering that the tire is flat on the road to independence. And so, instead of speeding towards freedom on the roads, you find yourself counting change for the bus ticket on your way home, hoping that your father will keep paying you.

This odyssey to the much-desired driver's license is a comical reminder of how choices, even those that seek the much-desired freedom, often place us at unexpected crossroads. The money invested, which could have given us the glamor of driving, turns into an ironic lesson about the true costs of independence. And, as we smile at the twists and turns of this chapter, we remember that, in the great "War of the Pockets", every decision, no matter how simple it may seem, contributes to the rich tapestry of our financial lives. After all, even the choice between taking a bus and driving reveals nuances of the eternal battle between the Today Me and the Future Me.

University - Hormones rising, pockets falling

At the epicenter of university competition, pockets, often anchored in parents' resources (after all, they are the ones who pay for the tuition), observe the frantic search for the top, where ostentation dictates the rules.

In this academic scenario, where hormones are boiling and financial resources seem scarce, we find ourselves in an arena of competition that rivals the most intense disputes. The race for the title of "best car" sparks a silent competition in college parking lots, turning vehicles into status trophies in an ongoing battle. The same occurs in the field of technology, where the competition for the best cell phone turns the corridors into catwalks of shiny devices, displayed as true works of art.

Competition is not restricted to the mere accumulation and display of material goods. The spotlight also turns to who wins the most attractive partner and even who had the best vacation trip. Academic life unfolds like a constant spectacle, where each victory is celebrated like a trophy on the shelf of social validation.

However, competition goes beyond traditional achievements and permeates all aspects of university life. From choosing to save money on lunch to afford a box at the college party to exchanging the "top" drink for a more affordable option to guarantee more quantity than quality, financial decisions become an integral part of this competition. Even outside the limits of college, choices that impact the wallet are made, always with the concern of maintaining status and ostentation.

Thus, the battle continues to write its chapters at this stage, where financial choices are shaped both by the search for social recognition and by the need to balance the student budget. College life, full of extravagance and bold decisions, turns into a unique financial comedy, with laughs that will echo for a long time in the big book of the "War of Pockets".

As we close this tumultuous university journey, we understand that the financial decisions made during this period have a lasting impact on our future path. The competition, ostentation and financial challenges do not disappear with graduation, but they continue to influence our path.

Choosing to prioritize temporary experiences, sacrificing quality for quantity, or giving in to social pressure during college can have significant consequences. Some may face financial difficulties post-graduation due to a high standard of living maintained throughout their degree, while others who have adopted financial discipline see a smoother transition to life after university.

The balance between enjoying the present and planning for the future becomes clearer. The "War of the Pockets," shaped by college experiences, is not just an isolated chapter, but a legacy that continues to influence our financial choices. Each decision, no matter how trivial it may seem, contributes to the unique narrative of our financial lives, influencing the path beyond our academic days.

This passage about "Adulthood," obtaining a Driver's License, and competing in college provides several lessons regarding expectations versus perspectives:

Life stage	Expectation	Perspective
"Adultization"	Clear transition to financial independence.	Complexity of adult life, balancing autonomy and financial support.
CNH (Driver's License)	Key to total freedom.	Independence from driving, but financial realities can complicate achieving freedom.
University (Competition)	Life is associated with competition for material status. It is social.	Financial choices as part of the competition, requiring a balance between social validation and responsible money management.
Lasting Impact (post-formed)	Job with a good salary, a successful relationship or marriage and lots of travel.	Financial choices during college have lasting impacts, highlighting the importance of a long term perspective.

This table highlights the differences between the expectations initially conceived at each stage of life and the real perspectives revealed by the text, highlighting the importance of a conscious and balanced approach to the complexities inherent to the financial journey.

Part III: The mountain peak, the culmination of financial choices and challenges

Welcome to Pico da Montanha, the stage of life where we gain greater authority over our choices and, theoretically, enjoy greater purchasing power. In this chapter, we'll explore the nuances of the professional world, the social pressures that shape our behavior, and the daily decisions we make as we face the challenge of balancing professional success, personal satisfaction, and the lessons learned from past financial battles. The "War of Pockets", and people's lives, reaches its peak, where purchasing power increases, but freedom and time become precious resources.

In the hallways of the professional world, we are faced with the unique duality of having more control over our lives, while simultaneously facing the pressure of devoting the majority of our time to careers that seek higher pay, workplace validation, and potential advancement. professional.

Amid 80% of our lives dedicated to work, we chase not only a better salary, but also the approval of superiors, co-workers, social circles, family and friends, incessantly seeking the much-desired promotion after validation. All of this unfolds in a scenario shaped by influences from early childhood to intense experiences at university. Here, at Pico da Montanha, financial decisions are made in an environment full of previous learning, where each person carries emotional baggage that directly interferes with our choices and decisions, and they reflect not only on our present, but also cast shadows and lights on the future.

Workplace

When it comes to adult life, it is inevitable to observe how this battle extends to the corridors of the workplace. The never-ending quest for social validation, which began as a "work with you love" narrative, has infiltrated our professional lives in unexpected ways.

Just as we worry about what we wear and use on social media, the same dilemma permeates our choices at the office. Ah, that colleague who seems to be the official ambassador of technology and fashion at the office - always parading around with the latest gadget and trendy corporate dress code. It kind of becomes our unwitting guide to what's hot. The pressure to maintain an impeccable professional image sometimes makes us spend as if promotion depended on the latest laptop model. Who would have thought that career advancement would also include a technology parade, right?

Furthermore, the workplace has also become an arena where competition for financial and professional success is intensified. Constant exposure to colleagues' achievements on social media can create a silent race for the next promotion, the next bonus, or the next extravagant trip, leading to financial choices that aim to impress rather than sustain balanced financial health.

Parenthetically, we are faced with a situation that few people see, where we spend resources that we often don't have to acquire things that are not essential, all with the intention of impressing people who, in truth, don't matter to us.

How this subtly ironic observation resonates in everyday plots. Sometimes it feels like we're all acting in a peculiar comedy, where the plot unfolds between the incessant search for shiny objects and the frantic attempt to please an imaginary audience.

In this comical script, they make us smile at our own extravagance, questioning the logic of investing our hard-earned money in things that, in reality, they do harm the difference in our lives. It's as if we were participating in a popularity contest where the prize is... well, nothing very valuable, other than the fleeting applause (or sometimes just a crooked nose of envy) from those who might not even deserve effort.

So, while we try to resist the temptation to trade our car for a spaceship just to impress the neighbor, or not let ourselves be carried away by the compulsion to purchase the latest smartphone model, let us appreciate the subtle comedy of life. This reflection invites us to rethink our extravagances with a smile, as if reminding us that, after all, everyday comedy can be the best form of wisdom.

But returning to work, this battle in the environment is not just a question of status or exhibitionism, it is a manifestation of the conflict between the "Me of Today" and the "Me of the Future" in the professional context. As jugglers in this financial circus, we often find ourselves balancing between the social pressure of keeping up appearances and the need to make sound financial decisions to ensure future stability, and of course, without letting anything fall.

Therefore, it is vital to reflect on how we can redefine our priorities in the workplace, finding a balance between the search for professional recognition and financial responsibility. After all, true victory is not just in climbing the corporate ladder, but in ensuring that every step taken is sustainable and contributes to building a solid financial foundation.

The social circles

We also cannot ignore that this battle infiltrates social circles that are supposed to be for entertainment and leisure. The gym, the church, the clubs, all these places become battlefields where the fight between the "Me of Today" and the "Me of the Future" reaches new heights.

In social circles, the pressure to keep up appearances and participate in activities that are often beyond financial reach becomes an almost invisible reality. Modern society encourages us to attend environments and events that, although they promote social interaction, most of the time require a considerable financial investment.

The gym, in modern times, transcends its original purpose of maintaining physical fitness, transforming into a scenario where sportswear brands and gadgets and fitness items are not just accessories, but essential components of the experience (and their existence in the academy). What about digital influencers? They have raised expectations to unprecedented levels, leaving even those regulars who have witnessed the changes over decades surprised by the evolution of the scene.

Participating in a religious ceremony often resembles a spiritual fashion show, where the choice of attire is meticulously evaluated, sometimes receiving more attention than the depth of our spiritual connection. In this context, a peculiar irony arises: as we strive to nourish our souls and find spiritual meaning, we are simultaneously subjected to the pressure of maintaining outward appearances. This duality reflects in a humorous way the constant negotiations between our financial choices and social expectations, highlighting the comedy that surrounds our financial journey. Furthermore, the religious setting often becomes a stage for comparing clothes and jewelry among women and possessions among men, adding yet another layer of complexity to this subtle dance between our inner quest and outer demands, providing a Humorous look at financial choices shaped by social influences.

Even in clubs and leisure environments, the pressure to participate in events and travel can create a financial dilemma between having fun now and securing the future. It's as if, when seeking leisure, social enrichment, and even new connections, we find ourselves entangled in a web of expectations that often ignores our financial realities. The struggle to balance social participation with financial responsibilities turns what should be leisure time into another front in the war against shopping and status impulses.

So, while we face social interactions bravely, we also need to develop strategies to transform these environments into allies, where human connection is prioritized over material competition.

Workplace	Expectation	Perspective
Pressure on professional image	Pressure on Professional Image	Emphasizes the need to balance professional image with responsible financial choices.
Professional competition	Intensificatio n of social competition in the workplace.	It highlights the importance of making sound financial decisions, maintaining a balance between social pressures and financial responsibility.

Social Circles	Expectation	Perspective
Gym and lifestyle	Investment in brands and gadgets as an essential part of the experience.	It highlights the irony of investing in appearances while seeking well-being, promoting reflection on financial choices.
Religious ceremonies	Pressure to maintain outward appearances during spiritual events.	It reflects the duality between inner search and social expectations, offering a humorous look at financial choices.
Clubs and leisure	Financial dilemma between immediate fun and planning for the future.	It emphasizes the need to balance social participation with financial responsibilities, transforming social environments into allies.

These tables highlight early expectations in different areas of adulthood and the insightful insights that emerge from the text, emphasizing the need to balance social pressure with responsible financial choices and develop strategies to transform social environments into allies.

On this journey through the financial dance of life, we move in time with our monetary choices. Carefully examining essential and non-essential expenses, always seeking to maintain financial stability, allows us to find balance in life. Just like an orchestra, learning to compose a harmonious budget, where each component plays a vital role, leads us to a well-adjusted financial symphony, ready to face any challenge.

Setting financial goals with the determination of a tango brings us step by step closer to short, medium and long-term objectives. This journey, like a careful dance, will lead us to achieving these goals with focus and precision. Before taking the final step towards a significant purchase, a 24-hour reflective pause proves crucial.

This suspense allows us to assess the real need for this financial movement, ensuring that we are moving in the right direction.

By adjusting our financial outlook, detaching ourselves from negative influences, and reevaluating the accounts we follow on social media, we become empowered to shine without being obscured by unsustainable standards. The daily practice of financial gratitude becomes a synchronized choreography between us and abundance, reducing the weight of social pressures and focusing on what really matters.

In the job market, exploring negotiation opportunities is like bargaining at a street market. Evaluating professional benefits and seeking salary improvements puts us in a more favorable position, positively influencing our financial dance. Taking a financial selfie to reflect on our choices connects us with authentic movements that align our attitudes with financial goals.

Dedicating continuous time to financial education is like a perpetual rehearsal, transforming us into masters of the financial dance. Learning about investments, strategies and planning allows us to lead the show of our own lives with confidence and wisdom. Thus, we conclude that by dancing through life's financial nuances, we find not only balance, but also the art of thriving.

Children: Current gifts x future heirs

Another thing that we often don't plan into our lives, but that simply happens, is children. It's the time in our lives when our financial decisions not only shape our present, but also have a direct impact on the future of small versions of ourselves. Parenthood, a journey filled with joys, challenges and unexpected expenses, turns into a new financial chaos where careful planning is often challenged by the unpredictability of parenting. In this fascinating episode of our lives, diapers become investments, and each toy is a share in the stock market of family happiness.

As little ones grow, we face the pressing need to balance our children's voracious demands for desired items and our family's pressing financial needs. In this new stage, unexpected expenses take on even more complex contours, becoming choices that involve the desire to provide the best for children and the pragmatic reality of the family budget. If baby bottles were previously the epicenter of our concerns, now we are faced with incessant requests for state-of-the-art toys and other demands that rival the demands of the consumer market.

In this panorama of raising children, we understand that unpredictability persists as a rule, but now added with an extra pinch of challenges and laughter. Then arises the crucial need to find a balance between the desire to provide the "good and the best" for children and the responsibility to educate them in the best possible way, without falling into the trap of spoiling them. It's a delicate exercise in financial juggling, where choices reflect not only our values as parents, but also the impact that these decisions will have on our children's development and worldview. The challenge lies in being not only a provider of resources, but also a guide and mentor, preparing them to face the complexities of the world in a conscious and balanced way.

Creating an environment that encourages understanding financial choices allows children to absorb notions of budgeting, priorities and the importance of conscious decisions. Including children in discussions about family expenses, in an age-appropriate way, provides a more objective and in-depth understanding, and prepares them for the complexities of the financial world.

By practicing this balance between providing comfort and educating about financial responsibility, parents not only shape their children's worldview, but also cultivate essential skills that will be fundamental in their adult lives. Therefore, financial education in parenting is not just about numbers, but about providing the tools for future generations to navigate the financial landscape with wisdom and discernment.

We highlight the financial complexity that children introduce into their parents' lives, from unexpected expenses to choices that shape the balance between offering the best and maintaining the family budget. The lesson learned is the need to find a balance between meeting children's demands and respecting financial limits, teaching important values. The inclusion of children in discussions about family spending is also highlighted as a strategy to promote understanding and prepare them for the financial world in a conscious way. Financial parenting, therefore, goes beyond numbers, emphasizing the importance of providing tools for future generations to navigate the financial landscape wisely.

Expectations	Perspectives
Children may be ideally planned, but they often arrive without warningO.	Fatherhood and motherhood present unexpected financial challenges, requiring adaptation and balance.
As children grow, their wishes are readily met and the family's financial needs are not impacted.	As children grow, balancing their desires and the family's financial needs requires thoughtful decisions.
Meet your children's expectations, needs and financial goals without compromising the finances of your "today self" or your "future self".	The challenge lies in finding a balance between meeting your children's expectations and maintaining financial responsibility.
Children's education is sufficient only in common education, school and simple daily learning.	Including children in financial discussions provides an early understanding of budgeting, priorities and informed decisions.

Integrating financial practices into parenting can be an enriching journey for the whole family. By involving children in preparing the family budget, using interactive visual resources, we promote a deeper understanding of how money is distributed between essential expenses, leisure and savings. This exercise not only teaches you about finances but also strengthens family bonds.

Promoting hypothetical situations that require financial choices stimulates the ability to make conscious decisions together. These family conversations about available options and their potential impacts not only shape financial responsibility but also encourage a collaborative approach to solutions.

Implementing allowances responsibly is a practice that not only teaches about personal financial management, but also encourages autonomy in decisions. By setting savings goals and letting children decide how to use some of the money, we create opportunities to develop planning skills.

Including children in shopping activities, comparing prices and understanding value for money, contributes to financial awareness from an early age. Likewise, encouraging the collaborative economy between siblings promotes the notion of sharing and efficient management of family resources.

By planning leisure activities on a budget, families learn about choices and priorities. These experiences not only strengthen family ties, but also reinforce the importance of living within available financial means.

Encourage creative projects that allow children to earn extra money, such as selling handmade items or offering small services,promotes entrepreneurial skills and a deeper understanding of earnings and investments.

The practice of taking children to visits to banks and ATMs, explaining the practical operation of deposits, withdrawals and balance monitoring, provides practical knowledge about the financial system.

Including charitable actions in financial planning, setting aside a portion of the budget for donations and allowing children to choose organizations or causes to support, instills altruistic values and social responsibility.

By reflecting as a family after making a purchase, discussing the need for the product, avoiding impulsive choices and considering alternatives, we promote a culture of reflection and awareness in spending.

By doing this, not only will strengthen children's financial education, but they will also create a family environment where financial decisions are understood and made consciously. By involving children in decision-making, they will not only value the family budget more, but they will also be actively helping parents constantly evolve their financial approach.

Part IV: Reflection for the transition of the "future self"

Introduction to Transition

As we prepare to enter the crucial phase of transitioning from "Present Self" to "Future Self," it is imperative to reflect on the journey that has brought us here. Like an engaging financial plot, the previous pages of this book outlined the chapters of childhood, adolescence, university and adulthood, outlining the choices, challenges and achievements that shaped our relationship with money. This introduction will serve as the bridge that will lead us through the transition, connecting the past to the present as we prepare to face the challenges and opportunities that await our future. This transition applies to anyone, regardless of their stage in life, because when it comes to changes (for the better), it's never too late to start.

Glimpsing the "Future Self"

Building your "Future Self" starts by defining where you would like to be in 10, 20, 30 years, and your financial goals to achieve it. This involves clearly identifying what we want to achieve in the future and setting realistic and measurable objectives. We understand that, amid the challenges of "Today's Me", this task may seem difficult, but, on average, many share the desire to reach old age with comfort and financial freedom, transforming the narrative from obstacles topleasures. Imagine going to the beach or fishing whenever you feel like it, without having to ask permission or spend your precious vacation days. Planning trips without calculating how many vacation days are left or doing math like "work another 6 months to fix the air conditioning". It's this kind of financial freedom that makes the

"Future Self" journey so exciting and full of possibilities.

It is common to find ourselves wrapped up in grandiose aspirations about the future, fueled by expectations that are often exaggerated. We dream of stellar careers, financial stability and epic achievements, while reality insists on reminding us of its unpredictable nature. These humorous tables highlight the disparity between our optimistic expectations for the next 10, 20, 30 and 40 years and the cruel reality we often face. Between grandiose dreams and concrete actions, there is sometimes an abysmal gap, where hope often turns into an uninhibited wait for an unlikely miracle. Let's take a peek at this journey through the years to come and laugh a little at the unexpected curves that life throws at us.

10 years:

Expectation	Reality	Concrete Actions	Uninhibited reality
Get a promotion, keep your finances under control, have a comfortable apartment	Frequent job changes, saving to pay rent every month	Update CV on LinkedIn, watch online personal finance tutorials	Waiting for a raise that never comes, trusting that someone will solve your financial life as if by magic

20 years:

Expectation	Reality	Concrete Actions	Uninhibited reality
Stability at work, a modest home, having some money saved for emergencies	Frequent financial worries, trying to save for the future	Contribute to social security, look for investment opportunities, participate in professional development courses	Believing that one day luck will turn around and solve all financial problems

30 years:

Expectation	Reality	Concrete Actions	Uninhibited reality
Retire with financial security, contribute to social causes, maintain a balance between work and personal life	Uncertainty about retirement, sporadic contributions to social causes, overwork	Postponing long-term investment decisions, waiting for a promotion to start contributing more to social security	Believing that at some point something will happen to improve your financial and professional situation

40 years:

Expectation	Reality	Concrete Actions	Uninhibited reality
Travel the world with passive income, be recognized as a career leader, achieve inner peace	Growing concerns about retirement, facing challenges at work, questioning career choices	Seek financial advice, reevaluate professional goals, implement lifestyle changes	Imagining that the lottery could be the final solution to all problems, hoping for an unexpected career turnaround

As we delve into this satire of life, it's natural to ask: "Do I see myself reflected in this table?" Guess what, dear reader,This experience of ups and downs is shared by many.We all, at some point, face the gap between expectations and reality, between lofty dreams and the complexities of daily life. If you identify yourself, know that you are not alone. Sometimes the comedy of life lies precisely in these situations. So, take a deep breath, laugh at the twists and turns, and remember that while life can be unpredictable, our power to adapt is a constant.

And how to deal with all this? And is it worth it? These questions resonate when we are faced with the challenges and expectations in the transition from the "Present Self" to the "Future Self". Dealing with this requires a balanced and realistic approach. Amid the complexities of financial planning, it is essential to embrace flexibility and adaptability. Unforeseen events are inevitable, and often the ability to adjust course is as crucial as the original plan.

Is it worth it? Well, it's like being in a complicated relationship with your financial life – you love it, you hate it, but deep down you know you need to do your best. After all, the journey is more like a roller coaster, with its ups and downs, and less like an elegant parade. The real value is in the experiences along the way, and who knew learning how to juggle bills couldn't be so horrible?

Additionally, seeking professional guidance and continually educating yourself about finances are important steps. It is not necessary to face this journey alone. Financial advisors, specialized courses, and educational resources can offer valuable insights.

Therefore, when dealing with the complexities of financial transition, the key is to embrace the journey with confidence, learn from experiences, and strike a balance between financial discipline and flexibility in the face of unexpected changes. This approach, while challenging, can make the transition not only manageable but also rewarding along the way.

Part V: Retirement and financial freedom, dream or reality?

This is where we finally begin to reap the rewards of our choices along this winding journey of life. It's time to reflect on how financial health directly impacts the construction of the "future self". Imagine two contrasting versions: the person who diligently took care of their financial health, compared to the person who completely ignored any concerns about money, a regrettably common reality for many.

The first, like a master sculptor, meticulously took care of every financial decision. He didn't fall into the traps mentioned in the book, such as unnecessary possessions and status, he set clear goals, saved consistently and invested intelligently. This person is like an experienced navigator, adjusting course based on the tides of the financial market. Over the years, you have built a solid foundation of stability, allowing you to face challenges with confidence.

Today, that person who acted like a master sculptor of his finances reaps the fruits of his diligence and long-term vision. In your retirement, enjoy a comfortable lifestyle provided by years of consistent savings and smart investments. Her ability to adjust course over time protected her from financial storms, allowing her to face the golden phase of life with ease. You have a solid diversification of investments, a paid-off home of your own and, most importantly, the freedom to enjoy your time without excessive financial worries. This person exemplifies how disciplined financial choices can result in a stable and rewarding retirement.

The second person, regrettably, treated his finances as an insignificant detail in the vastness of existence. He ignored goals, disdained savings and danced recklessly in the dangerous waters of uncontrolled debt. This approach is like an unwary captain who sails without a plan, sometimes navigating stormy seas without a guiding light.

Unfortunately, this person who overlooked his finances as an insignificant detail now faces the consequences of this reckless approach. Now, as he retires, he faces significant challenges. Lack of planning resulted in inadequate resources for retirement. Instead of enjoying the years of rest, you deal with accumulated debt, financial uncertainty and regrets about not making more conscious decisions in the past. A lack of financial direction throughout life resulted in an unstable and complicated retirement.

Comparison between two financial approaches

Aspect of Life	Financially Conscious Person	Financially Neglectful Person
Home	He has his own paid-off home, providing housing stability.	Face the possibility of rent or housing-related difficulties due to lack of estate planning.
Health	He invested in health insurance and preventative care, enjoying robust health.	You may face challenges due to limited resources for medical care and possible health concerns due to financial stress.
Travel and Leisure	You have the freedom to enjoy travel and leisure activities, benefiting from financial stability.	Limited in travel and leisure options due to budget constraints and constant financial concerns.
Children's Education	He offered his children a solid education, investing in their future opportunities.	You may face challenges in raising your children due to financial constraints, impacting future opportunities.

Food	Maintains a balanced and accessible diet, prioritizing health	You may face restrictions in the quality of your diet due to poor financial choices, affecting your health in the long term.
Quality of life	Enjoy a high quality of life, with access to comfort and opportunities.	Faces a reduced quality of life due to financial limitations, impacting access to necessities and luxuries.
Mental Wellbeing	Maintains an emotional balance due to financial stability and less stress.	May face chronic stress and anxiety due to constant financial challenges, affecting mental well-being.
Personal developme nt	Invest in personal development, exploring hobbies and seeking continuous growth.	Limited in personal development opportunities due to financial constraints and lack of resources to invest in personal interests.
Relationshi ps	Enjoy healthier relationships due to stability and less financial stress.	You may face tensions in relationships due to financial conflicts and constant worries.

Retirement	Enjoy a comfortable retirement with enough resources to support a desired lifestyle.	Faces financial difficulties during retirement, depending on minimum pensions and insufficient resources for basic needs.

The contrast is evident when we look at the "future selves" of these two people. The first reaps the rewards of a disciplined financial journey, enjoying stability, freedom and security. Meanwhile, the second finds herself sunk in debt, facing constant financial challenges and regretting the negligent decisions of the past.

So the lesson is clear: As we carve our financial future, each choice shapes the destiny that awaits us. Careful attention to financial health is like a constant investment in our own prosperity, providing a smoother, more rewarding path forward. Regardless of the current situation, the journey to a more prosperous "future self" begins now, and today's choices will resonate for years to come.

Helping to understand what 'financial freedom' is is essential, as most people do not even know the term, and rarely seek something that is unknown to them. Imagine financial freedom as a state in which your personal finances do not dictate your choices, but rather enable you to achieve your goals and dreams. To illustrate, consider the example of Ana.

Ana, a tireless worker, realized that her life was an eternal juggling act of paying bills and trying to balance her finances. The saga began when she decided to face the situation head on. Ana did a kind of 'X-ray' on her accounts, and look, the diagnosis was not encouraging at all. There was a bill that she didn't even know where it came from.

Ana's first step was as practical as the bread line. She cut expenses that were beyond unnecessary, like a wardrobe full of clothes that only served to keep moths company. Ana went on a real financial diet, but calmly, she didn't have to give up the sacred cup of coffee.

The comical part of the story was when she decided to enter the world of investments. Ana, who thought that only financial market tycoons did this, realized that her money didn't need to stay moldy in the bank. No, she didn't become the wolf of Wall Street, but she understood that money can be more useful than a screwdriver in a carpenter's hand.

The turning point was when Ana realized that financial freedom is not just for those who have three surnames. She started making decisions that didn't involve choosing between buying food or paying for electricity. It was more or less when she understood that money could be an ally, and not just an enemy that appears at the end of every month.

The turning point in Ana's journey was when she realized that she didn't need to work just to pay bills, but to achieve her dreams. Financial freedom did not mean having an exorbitant fortune, but rather having control over your finances and directing your money to work in your favor. This change in mentality was crucial to achieving financial freedom.

Over time, Ana wasn't just eliminating debt, she was building a path to financial autonomy. She chose to take a sabbatical to travel, investing in meaningful experiences that went beyond the limits of the traditional budget. For Ana, financial freedom meant more than having money, it was the ability to shape her life according to her personal aspirations, without being tied to financial restrictions.

This real-life example highlights how financial freedom is not a one-size-fits-all formula, but rather a personalized process. Every step Ana took, from understanding her finances to changing her mindset regarding money, was essential to achieving financial freedom. This illustrates how this concept goes beyond numbers in a bank account, being a journey of self-determination and personal fulfillment.

The Kingdom of Financial Freedom and Lasting Peace

I invite you to visualize your own kingdom of financial freedom, after all, dreaming doesn't cost anything. Think about your plans when you reach this state. What would be your priorities? What would your life be like with choices not limited by financial constraints?

Imagining yourself in the very realm of financial freedom is giving wings to creativity and envisioning a reality where the constraints of money no longer dictate the direction of life. In this realm, dreams become goals, and goals become achievements. Financial freedom is not just a concept, but the construction of a personal world where choices are guided by the most intimate desires, without the constant shadow of the budget. Here the plans take on new dimensions.

Visualize yourself dedicating time to passions that have always been put on the back burner. Maybe it's learning a new skill like writing a book, diving into creative projects, or even exploring a professional field that has always seemed distant.

Financial freedom also provides the opportunity to explore the world, without looking at your bank statement with trepidation. Travel becomes more than just a vacation, it is an enriching journey, opportunities for growth and discovery. Whether visiting distant cultures or exploring your own country, each destination is an extension of your realm of financial freedom.

In achieving financial freedom, there is also the power to make a difference. Contributing to social, environmental or philanthropic causes becomes not just a desire, but an achievable ability. Your financially free kingdom is a center of positive influence, where prosperity is shared and extended beyond your own boundaries.

Finally, in financial freedom, living without the burden of debt is liberating. Your kingdom is built on solid foundations, without the constant worry of outstanding debts. It's a life where each new day is welcomed with the certainty that your choices are not being dictated by your financial past.

So imagine yourself in this personal realm of financial freedom and allow these plans to become more than mere visions. They are the fuel that drives the journey towards a future where financial freedom is not just a dream, but a tangible achievement.

Final reflections on the importance of financial education

Now that we've reached the end of this book, let's take a look at those final tips that could be game-changers for your wallet. Every bit of advice shared here has the power to make a hassle-free difference to your financial future.

Put your feet on the ground, don't compare with others

Remember that friend of yours on Instagram who always seems to be on vacation in Bali? Well, his reality may not be as glamorous as it seems. Keeping to yourself and not comparing yourself to others is the key. Everyone has their own journey.

If You Don't Understand, Don't Do It

If you're looking at a financial graph and thinking "what language is that?", you might want to take a step back. Understanding what is going on before acting is always a good idea. Don't be the impulsive hero of your own financial story!

Seek professional help, but not what you find on the Internet

Valuable advice is worth the investment. If you need help, go to a professional. But please don't follow any advice that appears on the internet. No trusting financial advice that has more emojis than numbers.

Small details, big achievements

Don't underestimate the power of details. Those small daily habit changes can turn into big victories in the future. Every cup of coffee saved is one step closer to that dream vacation.

Everyone has had to give up something for a greater goal, you are no exception

When reflecting on success stories, one constant stands out: sacrifice. Every person who achieved financial freedom had to give up something to achieve a greater goal. Recognizing that these sacrifices are an integral part of the path is vital to the journey towards financial success.

Be careful with what/who you follow on social media, as that influences you and messes with your head

Social media is like an amusement park, but sometimes the rides are scarier than the roller coaster. Be careful who you follow, as those photos of yachts could end up making you spend more than you should.

Ultimately, financial education is an ongoing process of learning, adaptation and self-discipline. These final reflections are a call to action, a reminder that each choice shapes the future. May these words serve as a constant guide on your financial journey, empowering you to make informed decisions and pave the way for a more prosperous and conscious life.

Message of encouragement to maintain financial discipline.

As we reach the end of this financial learning journey, I want to share some words of encouragement to stay disciplined and continue on the path to your "future self."

Never give up on your "future self". The path to financial discipline can be challenging, but always remember why you started. Your "future self" deserves every effort, every saving, every conscious decision. Persistence is the key to turning your dreams into reality.

Start today, don't leave it until tomorrow. Procrastination is a silent enemy. Don't delay the start of your financial journey any longer. Every small step taken today is an investment in your tomorrow. Start now and reap the rewards of this decision over time.

Use time to your advantage. Remember the popular saying: "From grain to grain, the chicken fills its crop." Just like small grains of sand form a beach, your daily financial choices add up over time. Be patient, persistent and let time work in your favor.

Construction is a continuous process. Understand that building a solid financial foundation is an ongoing process. Every balanced budget, every debt paid, every investment made is a brick in the construction of your financial future. Celebrate each small victory as it pave the way for greater achievements.

If you feel like "flaunting", always remember your "future self". In moments of temptation to overspend, reflect on the needs of your "future self." The temporary satisfaction of "splurging" may not compare to the lasting fulfillment of achieving your financial goals. Keep your focus on the long term.

In the end, it will all be worth it. Today's sacrifices shape tomorrow. Every conscious choice, every well-thought-out financial decision is an investment in your future success. At the end of the

www.ingramcontent.com/pod-product-compliance
Lightning Source LLC
Chambersburg PA
CBHW071100290526
45795CB00004B/1585